T0129267

The Wedding Is WHO YOU WANT... The Marriage Is WHO YOU GOT!

THE WEDDING IS WHO YOU WANT... THE MARRIAGE IS WHO YOU GOT!

The Dating Companion Handbook

G. BALLARD JR.

THE WEDDING IS WHO YOU WANT... THE MARRIAGE IS WHO YOU GOT! THE DATING COMPANION HANDBOOK

iUniverse books may be ordered through booksellers or by contacting:

iUniverse
1663 Liberty Drive
Bloomington, IN 47403
www.iuniverse.com
1-800-Authors (1-800-288-4677)

ISBN: 978-1-5320-0979-2 (sc)
ISBN: 978-1-5320-0980-8 (e)

Library of Congress Control Number: 2016919417

Print information available on the last page.

iUniverse rev. date: 01/06/2017

CONTENTS

FOREWORD

This book has not come about from my professing to be nor from my believing myself to be an expert or spiritual authority on marriage ... by ANY means! It comes rather, as a result of reflecting on observations and corresponding thoughts and meditations on marriage and relationships I've come to know. After being left to raise a one year and few months old daughter in my twenties, then soon after becoming divorced, to now being remarried for close to 18 years, to having performed dozens of weddings, having conducted countless premarital counseling sessions and numerous marital mediation sessions, and to the witnessing of many divorces, I am more than just casually acquainted with the institution of marriage. I have decades of experiences from which I have gleaned and reflected from that qualify me to share some real life perspectives and quantifiable conclusions.

It is my hope that this dating companion mini-book accompanied by corresponding prayer(s), will assist you in meditating DEEP DEEP WITHIN, as you ascertain whether or not you're fully aware of and capable of successfully holding the <u>office</u> of a Husband or the <u>office</u> of a Wife and whether or not you are able and willing to perform the offices' required duties, commitments, laws, and functions!

That was a lot you say (or think to yourself) ... LOL ... you may have no idea!

Let's get to work ...

–Gary Ballard Jr.
Author

CHAPTER ONE

WHERE THIS ALL BEGAN ...

I can remember as early as Junior High School beginning to inwardly think that it was very strange how badly I wanted to be a husband and a father. Not right then of course, but I did want life to kind of accelerate so I could "get on with it" and build a family of my own. By this time I had these thoughts almost monthly and by the time I entered High School I was somewhat questioning inwardly why I was having these strong, recurring impulses?

It caused me also to remember that from a little boy I did have a real fondness of babies ... their little hands and feet, those tiny little fingers and toes, their baby breath, and INTENT gaze upon what they'd fixate on ... I'd wonder what baby thinking "sounded" like to them, and what their little figuring and deliberating sounded like? Apparently so fragile and limited yet so "potentially functional."

My curiosity of them was undeniable, especially when I'd see parents of those I knew with babies when they'd be inconsolable.

All of that crying and refusing to be comforted would draw me to wherever their cries rang out as I mesmerizingly watched their parent(s) try to appease their little cries. I would always offer my 8, 9, and 10 yr old services (or lack there of in case they needed a mind/personality a little younger and more relatable to their little one "I thought to myself " and then would express smh.)

I assisted in these moments so often that I actually got better than good at pacifying the little ones … even at that young age of mine! You can imagine the looks I'd get telling grown women "here … let me help you with him/her."

So by the time I was a freshman in High School I would tell parents/caretakers of inconsolable babies to hand them to me and not to worry … because I had "Super-Human Fathering Skills" 😐 😊 Where that was coming from I had no idea! LOL however, I DO NOW! I repeated that phrase often enough that I began to question myself, "where was I getting all of these "foreign" thoughts and peculiar phraseology or idioms from?" But I did know that I could do the job … and often did, many times to the absolute shock and awe of both my contemporaries and seniors!

I simply did what I saw them do so many times, being just as intent on the baby as the baby would be when trying to focus and look upon us in kind. Not by simply making baby noises no … I would ask them specifically what was the matter, gazing intently upon them trying to connect ... and in all eventuality most times did! So voila, another forever friend added to my little young shortlist lol! So back to mischievousness I went! LOL

What does this have to do with the subject of marriage you may be thinking by now? Quite a bit really ... being that procreation and/or parenting are in most cases, eventual in and to the marital union! It is foundational so to speak, in marriage.

An absolute mountain of consideration and attention must obviously be given to the possible rearing of children in the relationship.

This subsequent party (interrupter & its possible subsequent siblings) to the "Floaty Love Affair" of you "Rom-e-ante" and you "Juliet-tisha", is going to cause Q U I T E the different circumstance once your little "bouncing bundle of joy" ☺ arrives on the scene!

In all severity ... consider how many relationships don't weather the addition(s) and adjustment(s) and end ... in divorce, written or ... Un-Spoken! Yep ... I'm suggesting that age old reality of those you and I know of and have heard of, remaining "legally" married, to "Keep Up Appearances", yet emotionally and relationally divorced behind the closed, private quarters of your ... I mean THEIR ... "House". Or even waiting until all the children have "left the nest" to call it quits and make public, the private divorce they've been living out behind closed doors for however long. So sad ... So heartbreaking ... So tragic ...

CHAPTER TWO

GROW'N UP ...

For whatever reason, as a boy and then as a teen, I would find myself paying close attention to married couples. My father in particular was constantly having dinner parties and/or "entertaining" at his and my stepmother's home, and I would intuitively study random couples' interactions with one another (when allowed to be in their presence just long enough to greet them and/or to be "presented" to them before being banished to either the basement or upstairs for the next 6 or so seemingly life-long hours lol).

I'd for some reason always recall the differences in how the couples would look at each other, dote over each other, laugh with each other, be touchy with each other etc..or not!

This "perceiving" of mine ... if brought up by me, would get me hit with the all too well known rebukes in our culture; those being: "Stay out of grown folks' business", "Quit meddlin", "You better quit being Mannish", "Shut up and mind your business" etc ... LOL ... hopefully you're "singing along with me" right about now and chiming in with some of your own LOL!

I still have that "perception" today and it has been an <u>indispensable</u> "tool" in my life! It took my "Born-Again" experience in my sophomore year in college at Southern University in Baton Rouge, LA for me to understand what I actually had!

I learned that what I had/have is often called in "Churchdom", being "keen" and biblically known as one who is "discerning." The "Born-Again" experience has answered thousands of questions I've had all of my life such as why I was the way I was, and why I am "wired" the way I am. It (the "Born Again" experience) has done so for the countless other millions who have answered God's call unto them for an intimate relationship with Himself, their Creator ... the singular Creator of all that is! But that subject obviously is for a different book ... sorry I regress! 😊

So from as early as adolescence, the vast majority of us humans are prone to "show" or "flash" many of the "shall-be(s)" of our personalities as I did then. Hundreds of those "observations" that I made as many as 30+ years ago, are still vividly memorable to me today!

Those early observations ... and those I made of my own mother and father even before and after their

eventual divorce, shaped one by one my desires, hopes, and dreams of what my adulthood would look like ... just as your earliest to your current experiences have probably done for/to you!

I deduced and concluded that I wanted to be HAPPILY married! FOREVER! That I NEVER wanted my children to experience their God given childlike happiness and, their God given childlike joy, *extinguished* as the collateral and <u>UNAVOIDABLE CONSEQUENCE</u> of divorce!

The consequential ugliness of my parents' divorce had me studying to "fix" and "right" things for myself and others far too prematurely for me to even in part, be considering, especially at those various and untimely junctures in my life. Although none of my experiences would be wasted ... although I was already discerning ... I was *"mind-full"* of subject matter that <u>WAS</u> <u>NOT</u> <u>AGE</u> <u>APPROPRIATE</u> for me ... neither was it "cute!" This also consequentially had me ALWAYS pursuing and engaging in relationships that were INAPPROPRIATE on all kinds of levels!
From elementary school days on up ... always trying to be "Boo'd Up" with some girl smh ... "Talia" "Marti" "Corey" "Angel" "Ms. Adora" yes ... smh ... "Ms. Adora" and even "Ms. Sharon", all elementary school age crushes and so-called girlfriends ... smh again, I won't even fill up twelve more pages to mention Junior High, High School, and College "Interests" and "Participations" as to keep this book PG! Smh ... again ... (Look at you all nosey for more "deets") Lol

Anyway ... needless to say my errant behavior was largely a consequence of the "broken home" I grew up in and the resultant fissures and voids it caused in my heart and soul. I'm in no way blaming my parents for their decision(s) in my rearing, as I of course, like all humans, had/have a God given governor in my conscience that speaks to me of right and wrong. Like so many others, I ignored the warnings and misgivings and I did contrary to what was the best for me! To this very day some memories still cause me internal shame and regret.

It's amazing how much of our current day to day personalities and character express in some way or another our past experiences and, either their perceived consequences or rewards from those past impressions! We, as candidates for marriage, bring these intermittent "expressions" with us directly into the relationship.

So much of what is discussed in premarital "negotiations" as desires and/or "deal breakers" are a direct result of one's past experiences. From the simple opinion on what marriage really is and means "these days," to what constitutes grounds for divorce in one's opinion, to how many children (if any) are desired, the role(s) and frequency thereof of each candidate's extended family, desired joint annual income, type of housing and transportation, geographic location of residency, desired verbal and physical intimacy, desired time spent together, desired communication levels and types, etc ...

Again, so much of these unique desires have been arrived upon and deduced from each party's unique personal experiences, exposures, impressions, and observations. You're getting some of his or her past in your present and future together!

It is dire that you spend serious and severe, focused time and energy in critical discussions, exchanges, and/or **"NEGOTIATIONS!"**

CHAPTER THREE

NEGOTIATIONS...

*"It is dire that you spend serious and severe,
focused time and energy in critical discussions,
exchanges, and "negotiations"!*

The dating and engagement stage of relationships always is portrayed as the "floaty" "lovey dovey" "googly-eyed" phase when we're sooooooo in love and no time spent together is long enough, yadda yadda yadda ... when actually, the more serious and intimate the relationship gets, the more this phase should look sometimes like a couple of attorneys attempting to broker a highly hostile and contested deal, and at other times an intense interrogation! Lol

In all seriousness it should! For instance, I've observed in "Christian Circles", couples "leading off" with the "changed" person that they are now and have become being that they've "found the Lord". I'm not trying to be facetious … really I'm not … as I said earlier, millions have experienced the authentic Born-Again experience and its subsequent transformation of mind, body, and soul! Even if that is your claim or the claim of your mate, you/they are still a work in progress and will be until your/their "dying day." That being the case, at times the "needs more work" portion (lol) of their personality will present itself for your engagement and entertainment pleasure.

You have no idea how long you may have to either suffer or enjoy these varying "expressions" of your "booger-bears" personality so you'd be well admonished to be prepared to "deal" for as long as …

I have and do counsel couples to get the honest, most graphic and horrific, low down, gut bucket details of their new found "most loved ever of their life" ☺ because that could just be who walks in the door some Friday nights … or not … until late Sunday night perhaps! So many times husbands or wives have claimed to have been lied to or "duped" by their "suitor" because that person engages in some type of behavior they never shared that they've manifested at times, or said that their religious enlightening had delivered them from, or that they hate and would NEVER commit because of prior adolescent exposures, or perhaps had never before even considered displaying or participating in.

Whatever the excuse and/or causation, the other party is left to now deal with and negotiate what their response, if any, should and/or will be! It's amazing how these "Jeckle and Hyde" types of outbursts can cause those lovey-dovey lenses to fall right off of those eyes and reveal to you an absolute monster that you can't believe you ever imagined marrying!

Did you not consider that the things revealed to you in the interrogations were quite possibly, in some measure or another, still in your partner and a forever part of their psychology? Even if in nothing more than in their conscious or subconscious mind? Did you not recognize the corresponding emotions that were accompanying the conveying of their experiences and resultant consequences and effects on their volition?

Some VERY VERY difficult questions must be asked and answered by "Bae!" (Insert facetiousness)

(1) Ask them of their earliest childhood memories and how fond they are or not of them. This you'll see has shaped some if not a majority of their ideas on how they will or will not parent "their" child(ren).

(2) Discuss sexuality ... DISCUSS SEXUALITY! DISCUSS ... DIS-CUSS ... 🙊 Inquire about their earliest experiences with sexuality. Observed? Participations? Experiences? Exposures? Then ultra importantly, with each of those, the accompanying emotional takeaways from those accounts. You best be assured that you might entertain the affected part of their personality when dealing with your partner's sexuality (or

lack thereof) at some time or another in the 60+ years of the "til death do us part" journey you're embarking upon together! This too, you'll find, will have a tremendous influence on the "why's" of how your mate will parent! For example, sleepovers or not, and why or why not!, just to mention ONE example!

(3) Discuss Finances! Once again watch how fast the past of one's life will be brought up as to how the person has come to qualify just how they've decided what is and what is not going to be comfortable and acceptable (or not) for their impending life together with you! Do you agree with them? What kind of dwelling do they want to live in? How many dwellings and where? To rent or to buy? Until when and for how long? How large or small of a dwelling and why? A yard or no yard? How much garage space and storage space, and to house what? How many bedrooms and why? Large kitchen and dining area or small? Mansion or condo? Studio or efficiency? Again, where and for how long!? How many times have you heard of people saying that what **they** want for **themselves** and **their** children is based on what **THEY THEMSELVES** did or did not have "growing up"? There again ... their past sitting at the table of YOUR PRESENT and YOUR FUTURE! Hmmm ... How much will the two of you travel and where to if at all? What types of foods will you prepare or purchase to

share together? In what room of the house, at what time, and on what type of furniture will you share it on? Oh yeah? How often? What kind of clothes will he/she wear, where will he/she purchase them, for how much, and how often!? With whose money? What types of transportation will you use, and for how much? How often? For how many years of your marriage will this be the case or usual mode of transportation? With whose money? This list is unique to every couple, with their own unique tastes and desires and it will grow infinitely as you go through day to day seconds, minutes, hours, days, months, and years together! Your boo-boo's knees may not be able to pedal that bike back and forth to work forever!? With their "GREEN" self! (facetiousness inserted) So obviously in just these very few and obvious life "dictates" a commensurate amount of income is required to facilitate these varying stages and seasons of desired lifestyle in the marriage. So both of you take your hands off of each other long enough to ... DO THE MATH!

(4) What about parenting? How many children do you want if any AND WHY? What about your boo over there? How many does he or she want AND WHY? "Why" matters because I want you to again recognize just how much the "past" of our lives has influenced our present and future desires! Will the two of you rear your children on Natural milk or formula? Says who? Why?

How will YOU discipline your child(ren)? What about them over there? So to each of you, where did your planned method of teaching/correction/ discipline derive? What about school? Private, public, or home school? Why? What faith will you raise your child in if any? Why and or why not? Will your child(ren) wear the latest, trendy fashions or be modestly arrayed as not to cause them to be "bent" toward materialism, consumerism, or classism if one way or another can instigate or deter such? What about sports, the arts, recreation, friendships, post secondary education and career aspirations? What about their potential marrying one day? What if they decide to marry someone with a skin color or religious beliefs vastly differing from their own or either of yours? Again, this list will go on and on and on and with the love you'll potentially have for your offspring, and rightfully so! How in depth have your interrogatories and subsequent negotiations gone thus far in your deliberating marriage with one another?

This is a CRUCIAL AND CRITICAL stage of the "courting" process and with all of the discovery of information on your prospective mate, there will naturally come differences in opinions and desires which is why I keep emphasizing it as the "NEGOTIATION" stage!

You know ... to negotiate!? To be at an impasse thus causing you both to have to explain your position at times in hopes of causing the other to see your viewpoint and agree to adjust their "demands" to facilitate yours or vice versa? You know … negotiate? To perhaps forgo one or more of your desires to facilitate instead the wishes of the best thing since sliced bread you've found there???

You know since ALL **YOU** WANT TO DO is make them the happiest person in the world for the rest of their life! You know since ALL **YOU** WANT TO DO is enhance their life and make it better since the day they found you!..You know, as you've told them soooo many times that ALL **YOU** WANT TO DO is to see them happy! 😊 Remember all the late night soft talk on the phone? Oh I forgot … on the text? lol

This really is the most critical phase of courtship! This is actually the MAKE IT OR BREAK IT (off) stage. Or should be! If the two of you cannot agree on just these three of MANY critical topical matters, then perhaps you're incompatible!? That's not a cuss word, nor is it the end of the world so to speak to find this out! You can freely decide to end marital considerations and attempt then to negotiate on a friendship? I/We already know the conclusion to that discourse! Smh … oh you "besties" you!?!😄

I wonder what the participation–attitude is/was like between the two of you during this interrogatory phase? How much laughter if any? How much patience or impatience? How much anger and frustration if any? How serious did your partner take this stage? How flexible are they really? Did they compromise or not? *Did he/*

she really ever consider <u>your</u> happiness as future plans and desires were agreed upon or attempted to be agreed upon? How flexible or rigid are/were you? Did you see another "side" of them? Did you call them out on it? Did they get defensive, retaliatory, or did they concede? <u>Take some time to intensely reflect here!</u>

CHAPTER FOUR

SAY SOMETHING I'M GIVING UP ON...

This phase is also critical because this "negotiating table" will be visited countless times by the two of you as you partner, to ACHIEVE and DEFEND your agreed upon and desired happiness, joy, and best possible life together! The majority of time spent together between couples is not eating, drinking, sex, shopping, traveling, etc ... The majority of time spent together is in close quarters in conspicuous silence. There's nothing strange about that! When we leave our homes, with all electronics turned off..there's virtual silence for the most part. We (as people) bring the noise ... and rightfully so!

How quiet are deserted cities and towns whose factories have shut down, businesses closed, and residents moved on to other occupations? How quiet are empty buildings in our cities, and deserted houses and apartment buildings?

Can you imagine living in that kind of silence and obsolescence?

The vast majority of us enjoy friendships and seek intimate relationships to avoid or mitigate that very actuality and existence!

Then how futile would it be, to spend thousands and thousands of dollars, and hours upon hours of stress and anxiety, for a 20-30 minute ceremony, to wed someone who will do nothing more but be around to co-sign and bemoan the exact same mundane silence and boredom!?

Do you have any idea how absolutely fulfilling and exciting it is to have someone you can't talk enough with? Oooooh Wheeee, it can't be beat! Imagine being married to someone that you can "conversate" with as much as you do with your best friends! It exists! How often have you been to restaurants and witnessed couples sitting across from each other hardly muttering the slightest word to one another!? I wonder why they'd even get dressed and leave the house to do so. It looks so boring! Tortuous almost! Yet you put the same two people in the company of their peers and you'd have to ask them to keep it down in the same exact restaurant smh ... Too bad ...

I'd much rather be "tied" to someone that I enjoy having conversation with! To talk about the news of the day with ... you know ... the things that are going on in the world! To talk about the latest happenings in the family. What's going on with me or them in our places of business. How we might be feeling that day or the deep or humorous thoughts we may have had that day. Dreams, hopes, aspirations, and thoughts about the future! Ugghhh just some type of meaningful dialogue other than "Hey, Huh, Nah, Yep, Cuz, IDK, OK," Jesus save me!!!😵🙂

The more intelligent, intelligible, perceptive, and introspective you are ... the more you're going to HAVE TO MARRY a capable conversationalist! Please do not underestimate your capacity and necessity for mental stimulation! I GUARANTEE you that physical attraction(s) will become less and less perceptible as you find yourself trying to get mental stimulation and gratification out of a dullard! You'll find yourself restless, sleepless, and aching of heart for someone who can fulfill your need for mature, intellectual exchange!

If there's little awe inspiring verbal exchange and idea sharing now ... RUN!!! It's not going to get any better! Just worse! Perhaps you just don't have the same things in common and your partner's lack of conversation is highlighting that? Respect the deficiencies and don't "go over" them! Back up and deeply reconsider! Perhaps what's exciting and stimulating to you is just not in their "wheel house!"

WAIT!!! for the one you can walk and talk with, shop and talk with, drive/ride and talk with, excitedly share magazine and internet articles with, share similarly humorous jokes, emails and memes with! Someone you can sing along to the radio with, cozy up on the couch with, binge watch favorite tv shows with, press pause and make midnight runs for snacks with, meet in the middle of the day for lunch with, text with, miss when away from … ENJOY A SENSATIONAL FRIENDSHIP AND LOVE AFFAIR WITH!

CHAPTER FIVE

AWE'S OF ATTRACTION...

Don't ever diminish, or allow anyone else to diminish the importance of physical **and** "personality" attraction! There is nothing more NATURAL than someone being visually attractive and pleasing to the eyes! Again, from childhood we begin to recognize being attracted to the opposite sex and even begin to notice consistent "types" we are routinely attracted to, and then also consistent "traits" that we prefer.

DONT EVER SETTLE out of desperation and the pressure you may feel from family asking "how long are you going to take to settle down and find somebody?" or other peers who are seemingly getting married (and soon divorced) all around you! Settling on someone who you're not physically attracted to is one of the worst things you can do to the person you claim to care so much for!

There is somebody for everybody! Don't you dare rob your significant other of being someone's EVERYTHING

THEY EVER HOPED FOR! BECAUSE THEY ARE! They might not be your everything and more … but they are someone's, somewhere! God is able to cause a divine connection and get the two of them to cross paths … as long as you don't come along and steal and delay them, playing the role of "the interrupter!"

So what they have "admirable qualities" and you feel like they're "good enough" because you are impatient and haven't come across anyone better lately! You know, "these types right here with these kinds of jobs, making this kind of money don't come along very often!!!" You wretch you!!! Don't you do it! **THEY BELONG TO AND WITH SOMEONE ELSE!** Don't you rob them of the opportunity to feel what it's like to be truly loved, cherished, admired, doted over, anticipated, longed for, missed, celebrated, heralded, nurtured, lavished, and ravished!!! This is what their true love has in store for them! Not some "well they'll do!" Get away from them!

There's nothing worse than being with your husband or wife and seeing them look upon another (other than you) with astonied attraction, in ways they don't or perhaps never have looked at you! They will remember who/what they saw, so to the point that they will tell their friends of the "work of God's own hands"that they saw, just as soon as they get the chance to be away from you! 🐵 They can't wait to tell it actually! They may even have them on their mind when the lights go out in bed with you!

This isn't the first time their eyes have gone a shopping from you, and it won't be the last time either! This horrible, hurtful misfortune could've been avoided with just some honesty and patience! One of you letting the other know that you're just "not that into them" or that they're just not "your flavor!" THEN JUST WAIT! Fella, wait until you've accomplished the things necessary for you to accomplish, for you to fully attract, entertain, and sustain the "type" of female that YOU'RE attracted to! Quit running around town finding "objects of the now" to extinguish your little lust-fires out on until you land the "dime piece" you're really bent on having smh ...

Umm Ladies ... these days ya'll know that you're just as bad as the men (if not worse) in just using these dudes to get what you want, when you want it! You know "having your cake and eating it too!" "Getting the milk for free!" You know "Playette!" Gettin' these squares all geeked up at the mere miracle of spending some one on one time with someone as fine as you!? You know how "you be havin' em" right!?☺ YOU'RE WRONG! You know you ain't right! As bad as the fellas out there creating monsters! Because hurt people begat hurt people and you know it! Remember ... that's how you got this way! So, you oughta' go high five whoever hurt you (your trainer) and give him (or her) props for puttin' you up on game! You owe them really, 'cause they made you the cold, heartless Player/Playette you are!

Whether you my guy, are lyin' and schemin' for some sex, J's, trips ... or whether you ma'am, are using your aesthetic to pillage some "green as grass" lame outta' money, red-bottoms, bags, trips, bottles, etc ... you both are ruining the purity and objectivity of someone's future wife, husband, mother, or father! You're a cancer to culture!

All because you can't go sit down somewhere and wait to organically cross paths with someone tailored made for you! Someone whose looks you'd admire! Their walk, talk, cologne or perfume, hair, voice, body, conversation, outlook on life, aspirations, so forth and so on … ya feel me!? Someone who'd SATISFY your mind, body, and soul! Nothing in the world like this feeling!!!

Now this is the kind of person you look to spend your life with! Have kids with! Travel the world and experience new things with! Grow old with! This is the kind of relationship your heart and soul craves and will NEVER quit craving until it gets it! The wrong person (for you) WILL NEVER appease this incessant longing and demanding protest, bickering, and lamenting from your heart!

You know just the protest of the heart I'm talking about and so do the dates you've reluctantly gone on who heard the cries of your heart as well … Your eyes lacked intensity and focus when looking at them, your ears never really inclined unto their conversation(s), your mind never engaged their communication(s) and you never really reciprocated any thoughtful or heartfelt sentiments … because your mind was on other things the whole time anyway! It was just something to do … somewhere to go … you weren't doing anything anyway remember … just lookin' ahead at another bored day/night.

But what if it meant potentially so much more to them? What if they were/are reeeeaaaalllllyyyy attracted to you? What if they reeeeaaaallllyyyy like you? ALOT? Do the right thing! Let them know up front and early on that you yet have eyes for another, that you have yet to lay your eyes on! That hangin' out as friends is about all you can heartedly commit to! I believe God will bless you for it! Although it may hurt them a little because of the disappointment of what may never be, they'll remember you for it, and appreciate you for your honesty forever!

Don't forget to keep yourself in mind likewise, as once the object of one's infatuation! What was communicated to you as to what the "why's" were of <u>why</u> you were your admirers muse? Was it your eyes? Hair? Facial features? Legs, waist, etc … that contributed to your being just impassable and undeniable in their estimation!? Whatever the attributes were, **please respect the strength of their affectation on your companion!**

Over the course of years being married to my wife I gained (with her help) about 70 lbs. that I didn't have when we met and married. My waistline obviously changed, my face changed, the whites of my eyes darkened some, the skin around my eyes began to darken, my breathing got louder and snoring increased. Consequently my style of dress had to adapt, my sleeping pattern changed, my activity level with my children decreased dramatically, and I was not the most attractive expression of myself! Did she continue to love me and did I continue to feel love …

Yes! That's some of the reason why I was so comfortable being in discomfort perhaps.

I didn't like how I looked anymore and I just figured in approaching my 40's, perhaps this was the big turning point and it was proverbially "over for me"! Well it only took a couple of instances of being out in public and two guys, on two different occasions, (respectfully) letting me know how lucky a man I was to have such an attractive wife (I guess I'm Shrek I thought!) to inspire me to do something about this weight gain and get back to my "glory days." LOL

Well I did work on it for 2 and 1/2 years and rewarded myself on my 40th birthday with a 75 lb. weight loss - down to 175 lbs. My face looked again like the one my mom and dad gave me, I was able to look nicer in my clothes (being they're designed on a form, to a form), I had a restored healthy self concept, an increased activity level which benefits my young sons, and all that!

I did also realize it wasn't fair to neglect myself to the point of being less attractive to the woman I cared so much at one time impressing in many areas, including all I could do with my appearance! It wasn't fair that she was "stuck" with a little chunky old man that was once slim, trim, and meticulous, at least about his aesthetic! A renewed sense of responsibility has been awakened in me that I not only want to be my best self for me, but I also was a lot different looking when I got down on one knee and asked her to marry me!

The Wedding Is WHO YOU WANT...
The Marriage Is WHO YOU GOT!

I know you ladies might be cheering and Amen-ing those last couple of paragraphs.☺ I know you're side-eye-reading waiting for the boot to drop LOL! (WARNING:You Should Be! LOL). I know, I know your re-butt-al is already locked and loaded being you all bear our children ... yeah yeah we know, we know ... and concur! You're right! At the same time ... given this advent of reality TV, we are seeing both men and women losing 10's and 100's of pounds and inches at varying ages and stages of life ... so we're all capable of being more healthy and sustaining our aesthetic!

I counsel young men to keep well groomed! Keep a nice hairstyle and haircut! Brush your teeth waaaaayyyyy down in there!😄 LOL Keep that breath right!😁 Find hygiene products that are compatible with your body chemistry ... that are well able to slay all or your funk dragons! Wherever it may be that they lurk!☺ Do a push-up every now and then and walk/jog a little! Continue to look as much like the man your companion fell for, as much as is reasonably possible! If you're apart from each other during working hours ... be sure to look good and smell good for her when it's time for your time together! Don't give the "world" your best and come to her and leave her to settle with the worst!

Ladies ... ya'll too!!! We can't get you outta the bathroom and from in front of the mirror when you're getting ready to go out! To work or leisure or whatever! We wait ... and wait ... and wait ⌛😁 ... and then, Oh Yeah ... here she comes ... Ms. Amercia!!! BUT ... when your day is over

27

and you come home to your husband … there goes the face down the sink drain, off comes "hairs", nails, ahhh babe what happened to your lips? And why do your eyes look so squinty and far away!!!??? Bet your figure looks nice up under my old high school football jersey and sweat pants from 85! Ummm, so you had a garlic meatball sub on garlic bread with a garlic soft drink in the car on your way home huh!? Jesus be my friend 😩 … smh … LOL

Ya'll know it's not fair to take your best out of the door every day either … and bring home your oh so tired from the day self! We too as husbands have spent our day with others who took the time to present their best selves, only for me to come home to your worst?

We both oughta' commit to doing better! Why do we present our best to those to whom it matters the least!!!??? In most cases, complete strangers, who aren't paying us any attention anyway, nor are obligated to! We should want our spouses to be well pleased and satisfied with who and what is waiting on them at home! Don't forget your RESPONSIBILITY and FAIRNESS to your spouse!

So if/while you're unmarried remember, you like what you like. You're attracted to what you're attracted to. Have faith, be encouraged, enjoy your family and platonic friendships, your career and hobbies, and wait! Prepare yourself … for "THE ONE"!

CHAPTER SIX

JUST WHO DO YOU THINK I AM!?

I feel it safe to surmise that by now if nothing has been reinforced in this book explicit candidness has, as far as communication is concerned! The two of you must (regardless of how concerned you are with the collateral reaction from your significant other) be completely thorough and transparent in expressing your most sincere observations, thoughts, concerns, and even misgivings about one another!

Then to be fair … you must also be as transparent about yourself, and not leave all the figuring out and discerning to their being savvy and skillful enough to figure out the puzzle that you are! If they're not a practicing psychiatrist, they're more than likely gonna' need your help! How about being honest and totally bare before them as well?

There'll be nothing worse than to get a ways down the road in your relationship and they conclude you as a liar!

As you having had misrepresented yourself to them … you know, having played a good role long enough to have gotten what you temporarily wanted, when all you had to do was be as honest and forthcoming as you could be.

Make your expectations of them known:

I have a form I created entitled "Common Ground". It looks so simple and I love the looks that I get when I hand it out to couples considering marriage. A title on the top, a line down the middle of the page … "Husband" on one side, and "Wife" on the other. I provide each with a copy and tell them to simply fill it out until they can think of nothing else to fill the columns!

It's hilarious to me how nonchalantly they whisk away with their simple little pages and commence to filling them out, not knowing the volcanic eruption that is going to take place as soon as they're asked to hand them to one another for each others inspection! LOL I love seeing the expressions on their faces as they investigate each column over and over … each time more intently and introspectively than before! The big eyes, the frowns, the chagrin LOL …

Oh the conversations that all of a sudden arise! "You expect me as a husband to do what!!!???" "You think a wife should what!!??? Who do you think you're marrying??? Your mother or something!!!???" Oh I love it! Out of all the "yeah we pretty much covered everything, and know each other "like a book", and "we're ready to hit that aisle!" SMH ... Yeah, all until this simple little piece of paper enters the room!

It's critical then that you communicate JUST WHAT YOUR DEFINITION OF A SPOUSE IS ... AND EXACTLY WHAT YOU EXPECT OUT OF THE PERFORMANCE OF THE DUTIES OF YOUR SOON TO BE COMPANION!

Just what is your opinion of who a husband is and just what all he does?

Just what is your opinion of who a wife is and what all she is to do?

Just what is your expectation of your fiancé as a father?

Just what is your expectation of your fiancé as a mother?

What about as a son in law? Or daughter in law?

Or as a step-mother or step-father?

Please make sure you communicate expectations! This is how you save yourself from being accused in the future of having misrepresented yourself and, having it put out all over town how you lied and put up a big front only to be EXPOSED once you could no longer hide the real you now that you're in the "comfort of your own home" or "behind closed doors".

Do you have "quirky", "kinky", or even kinda' (or flat out) "nasty" little things you're secretly into practicing that you've been able to hide from them that know you casually or in the "friend zone"? It's only a matter of time then that you begin to try to hint around at introducing them to your spouse eventually *(you know little hints to see if they'll except it from or outta you, or perhaps partake in it with you … or slap you and leave you forever for that matter!!!???)* and if you continue to carouse about with your secret little vices you'll be sure to be discovered within the confines of marital cohabitation! So be a grown man … or a grown woman … and DISCLOSE AND DISCUSS THEM NOW! Otherwise, you risk paying thousands in attorney fees and divorce settlements and you pay for them later!

All that will be in addition to having your "business" spread all over town to shame you by your once beloved treasure, but now, despised divorcée. Oh and don't forget the "shall be public record" court transcripts! SMH … all because you two couldn't afford to be candid, patient, thorough, explicit, and honest? FOR FREE!!! SMH …

Please take it from me … the person who you think you can't live without … can be the exact person you could feel like you can't live in the same hemisphere with!!! HEAR ME … you can literally despise and curse the day you ever met them … and if you PROCREATE with them to boot … SMH … a world of regret, pain, hate, and loathing would be an understatement! You think this exploratory process takes some self work!!!???

Imagine the self work it'll take having borne children to this relationship only for it to fail, then having to work together for decades to come to co-parent? Perhaps you'll even have to deal with them bringing other of their soon to be partners into the mix with the two of you in your co-parenting … that could potentially be as crazy as you consider them to be!!!??? OH GOD …

So at this point the two of you (or just you) may think I'm the biggest "Hater" or pessimist in the world as far as marriage is concerned and that's fair, given the tenor of this little book! Therein lies the issue however! No one seems to want to get down and dirty UNTIL they're married and divorcing … which doesn't even have to be the case! Two people who are extremely attracted to each other, intelligent, intelligible, and are capable of cooperation, and commitment, with integrity, CAN HAVE A VERY SUCCESSFUL, MEANINGFUL, AND WONDERFULLY BLESSED MARRIAGE!

(See … some positivity from me 😄 ✋)

I pray you two deliberately mature your relationship into just that! That is of course the reason I took the time and put my own self out here to write this book! I've been "gainfully" married myself going on 18 years at this present time and, I love the comfort, predictability, and

G. *Ballard Jr.*

stability that a good, healthy, honest marriage affords! I want you to enjoy the same … and **so much more!**

May God bless the two of you as you honor His desire for man and woman to be joined in holy matrimony … and that until death (in old age) do you part!

Here's a prayer from me to you if you will …

Father God, creator of ALL that is in existence … thank You for our lives, thank You for Your mercy, long suffering, and gentleness with us and all of mankind! We acknowledge Your existence and power to do with what YOU WILL, all that exists … We confess Your goodness and grace thus far has been our experience with You and for that we thank You! Lord as the readers of this book sincerely prepare themselves for matrimony … I ask that You, through Your Holy Spirit, lead them and guide them to and through ALL TRUTH about themselves, their circumstance(s), their aptitude, capacity, and potential … as well as that of their love interest! Let them have an undeniable peace or grief in themselves as to whether or not this relationship will bless or harm them … let them have a knowing one way or another that they cannot humanly confuse nor ignore! Give them the strength of heart and soul to obey Your communicating to them to their own life-long benefice! I ask that You bless them with peace, love exchanges, joy, health, wealth, prosperity, and that You Oh our God would satisfy them with long life ... and life eternal in Your perfected world to come! I/We ask these blessings through the belief, trust, and thanksgiving to You that we have in Your Son, the Messiah and Christ that some call on as Yeshua ... or in the english pronunciation "Jesus", the anointed One. Amen.

Conclusion

Well … I feel a satiation in only bringing you thus far in your journey toward a happy, fulfilling, and inseparably fused bond of oneness you're beginning to forge together!

Thorough communication is the key and since this is only a companion/handbook, it's solely designed to instigate and facilitate a level of communication and DISCOVERY that is so often neglected in the engagement stage of the relationship which so often causes the onset of unbearable confusion, frustration, exhaustion, desperation, and ultimate separation of "very good friends."

This is so unfortunate because it just doesn't have to be! This is one of the major (but several) reasons why almost one half of the marriages in the United States end in divorce! It's amazing how two people who declare sooooooo much undying love for each other can later sit on opposite sides of attorneys' tables from one another, hating the day they ever breathed the same earthly air, and want nothing more than to forget the other ever existed!!

Amazing! The fate of so many smh! Save yourself the anger, the frustration, the disappointment, and embarrassment and take the time to do the hard work now!

It's my personal belief, after all of my experiences with marriages, that most marriages could/can make it! Depending firstly on each person's ability and willingness to execute the office/role of the husband and the wife, how selfless and forbearing the parties can/will be, and how committed they are to being and remaining to be the "personality" that the other fell in love with in the first place!

That's all that can reasonably be expected of anyone … to be and do, what they vowed and agreed they'd be and do! Ask questions and discover all the earthly information you can about the ONE you claim to love so much and desire to spend the rest of your life with.

Then with that information honestly deliberate your compatibility with and, if you just down right even like that person or not! Respect, value and appreciate that person or not. Are GENUINELY physically attracted to him/her or not. Will you enjoy or despise being in close quarters with that person for 15 or so hours a day for the rest of your life or not? In sickness? For poorer? For worse? Despising ALL others? Even your "momma-nem"? Even above your eventual children?

If you're willing to commit to the keeping of YOUR WORD and YOUR VOW … and can totally give yourself away to your love … then by all means …

GET MARRIED!!!

AND LIVE HAPPILY EVER AFTER!!!

DEDICATION

This book is prayerfully written to the honor of all of those that God has employed in making a tremendous investment of righteous instruction in me. When I was a teenager living a reckless teenage life, it was Bishop William Barlowe (my Father in the gospel), who through the gospel of salvation through Jesus Christ, challenged my lifestyle of reveling bringing me to denounce a lifestyle of sin and degradation. It was Juanita Bynum who graciously introduced me to Dr. Donald Curlin (My Spiritual Father), who would train me in the ways and lifestyle of the Kingdom of God that I could live a life pleasing unto my Heavenly Father. It was Mother Estella Boyd (my Spiritual Mother), who God would eternally grace me to be spiritually delivered by and imparted into, that I might be used by Him. It was Dr. Angie Ray who God would grace me to come into a most sacred covenantal relationship with, who would instruct me in the ways of deliverance and spiritual warfare while administering the same to me, in the spirit of the true Spiritual Mother that she was! She was also the first to allow me to contribute to a published work and for that, I am forever reminded, humbled, and grateful! Finally to

Dr. Gertrude Stacks, a living legend and a true Master Teacher who tirelessly continues to share and instruct me, my household, and those that I influence, in the glorious "High-Ways" of God's desired lifestyle for mankind while on earth! I am eternally thankful to you all and to God My Father for you all!

Printed in the United States
By Bookmasters